FELICITY YOUNG

BOSSINEY BOOKS

PLATE ACKNOWLEDGEMENTS

Front cover: Roy Westlake
Other photographs: Ray Bishop, Michael Deering
Drawings: Felicity Young

First published in 1990 by
Bossiney Books
St Teath, Bodmin, Cornwall

© 1990 Felicity Young
ISBN 09481 58 64 6

Typeset and printed by
Penwell Printers Ltd
Callington, Cornwall

ABOUT THE AUTHOR
and the book

FELICITY YOUNG is a Cornish-based painter who lives at Tintagel with her husband Ian, daughter Hazel and dog Arthur. She lived in Somerset for more than twenty years and still makes regular visits to the county, having first come to know Exmoor through childhood holidays at a farm high on The Quantocks.

She was educated at Lord Digby's Grammar School, Sherborne.

Since 1984 she has contributed over 200 illustrations for a whole range of Bossiney titles, covering six areas: Cornwall, Devon, Somerset, Avon, Dorset and Wiltshire. A member of The British Horse Society, she rides regularly and teaches Yoga. In 1989 Felicity made her debut as a Bossiney author, contributing a chapter on Lawrence of Arabia in *Dorset Mysteries*.

Now in *Curiosities of Exmoor*, she makes a fascinating tour showing that Exmoor has its fair share of rarities and wonders. Delving into history and folklore, the author reflects 'You can never be sure just what is around the next corner ...' The ghosts of Exmoor, the curiosities of its weather, its wild life, the red deer and the ponies are all featured, and many of the illustrations have been especially commissioned. This, Felicity Young's first title for Bossiney, is a must for all who love the mystery and magic of Exmoor.

EXMOOR – A JOURNEY OF DISCOVERY

E XMOOR itself is a Curiosity.
The moor holds a strange fascination, a magnetism drawing you to return time after time. You can never be sure just what is around the next corner: another secret valley, another hill to climb or a path to explore. Exmoor is full of mysteries just waiting to be unravelled.

Approaching the moor from Dulverton, which, says the signpost, is 'The Gateway to Exmoor', you feel you are travelling through a long dark tunnel, reaching towards a source of light in the distance, as you climb upwards through the trees twisting and turning, until eventually you burst into the daylight at the crest of the hill. In front of you are the wide open spaces of the moor. The familiar clatter of the cattlegrid heralds your arrival. Breath-taking views meet the eye.

All around is an ocean of wilderness, the copper coloured beech hedges which lined the route left behind; golden bracken, heather and gorse carpet the moor. Occasionally a tree, gnarled and bent double by the fierce winds, offers meagre shelter to cattle, sheep and wild ponies. Scanning the horizon you may glimpse ponies, or, better still, a stag. Overhead a buzzard hovers majestically, resting lazily on the thermal currents, rising high above the valleys where meandering streams cut their way into the hillside creating deep wounds in the otherwise rolling landscape.

Mystery lies ahead – over or under the bridge.

Walking up the track towards Dunkery Beacon, past Rowbarrows, on a beautiful winter's day it is difficult to imagine the hardships endured by a creature living on the moor. In the sunshine it seems a paradise. But how easily a fog can come down and envelop a traveller or a sudden snow shower obscure the path, and from striding out confidently one suddenly feels very vulnerable. The tumuli and barrows become suspicious mounds which could so easily harbour evil spirits, your destination, however far you walk, never seems to get any nearer. The moor can be a very frightening place – but also one of wonder and beauty.

Standing at the top of the Beacon by the stone cairn, the wind blowing fiercely, you can see right across the Bristol Channel to Wales, ships slide slowly towards their destination, the sun glinting on their hulls as they glide by. It makes one feel small, just a tiny speck in the midst of this vast land and seascape. How wonderful to be that bird soaring above looking down on the miniature figures walking or riding on the moor, the sheep and cattle appearing as dots scattered at random, or to

'the Exmoor hills from side to side'....

Lyrical Exmoor countryside

be, in the words of John Crisford, a highly regarded Exmoor poet, a
giant who would . . .'bestride

> the Exmoor hills from side to side,
> and with my great all-seeing eyes
> look down upon this paradise
> and stoop and fondly touch the sea,
> and kiss the cairn on Dunkery.'

Dunkery was originally a fire beacon. A bonfire on the 1704 ft high
summit enabled the alarm to be raised when invasion threatened, a
chain of fires being lit throughout the county as a warning signal. The
light from Dunkery could be seen many miles away. The cairn itself is
a huge heap of loose stones of every shape and size, presumably the
remains of the fire-hearths. This dominant feature is modern and set in
its side is a stone commemorating the gift of the hill to the National
Trust by Sir Thomas Acland, Bt., Colonel Wiggin and Allan Hughes,
Esq., in 1935.

Local people use the beacon as a huge barometer. When it is covered in low cloud it invariably heralds rain, hence the little ditty:-

'When Dunkery's top cannot be seen,
Horner will have a flooded stream.'

Another atmospheric rhyme which has been inspired by this remarkable corner of Exmoor was written by an unknown resident of Luccombe:-

'Grey and sad, grey and sad,
With a rain-wrought veil are thy shoulders clad;
Sad and grey, sad and grey,
Weird is the mist creeping up to-day,
Ghostlike and white from the stream where it lay,
Hanging a shroud o'er the lone wild way;
Hidden and still, hidden and still,
Who'll now come with me over the hill?'

Whoever the poet was he obviously knew Dunkery very well, summing up the awesome qualities of the place with these lines, but in his next verse he notes also its beauty:-

'Fair and bright, fair and bright,
Purple and gold in the autumn light,
Bright and fair, bright and fair,
The butterflies float in the warm, soft air.'

When I first sat down to research and write the 'Curiosities of Exmoor' I found myself reaching for the dictionary to look up the word 'curiosity'. Having been there many times and seen the well known, and the not so well known, places of interest, gleaned tales of folklore and become engrossed in the moor's unique atmosphere, I wondered what, from this multitude of things, would qualify for a chapter in a book about curiosities.

The Concise Oxford Dictionary was of very little help. It defines 'curiosity' as 'a strange or rare object', bringing to mind the Dickens' tale, 'The Old Curiosity Shop' or our latter day bric-a-brac stalls where one browses in the hope of finding a rare and valuable object. This definition did not satisfy my curiosity so I turned to the Dictionary of Synonyms and Antonyms and here I found my answer:- oddity, rarity, novelty, phenomenon, sight, marvel and wonder. Exmoor can be

'Who'll now come with me over the hill?'

described by all of these words, wonder at the scenery, marvel at the diversity in the landscape with its deep wooded valleys and open moorland. Discover a rarity in the Exmoor pony, the only true wild horse left in Britain, and oddity in ancient standing stones and earth-works, relics of early man's settlement on the moor.

Exmoor can boast phenomena in its tales of hauntings, and novelty in some of the rich folklore and sights that delight the thousands of people who visit Exmoor every year. Put together, these words encap-sulate an area of outstanding natural beauty now carefully preserved as a National Park so that it remains to be enjoyed by future generations. Some parts are enclosed to make best use of the agricultural land but the wild and the tamed can be seen side by side: a harmony existing between man and nature.

A curious phenomenon becomes apparent as you venture into Exmoor, all around the earth, the houses, the cattle, take on a red hue, even a grey pony seen grazing thoughtfully in its field appears tinged with pink, everything is affected by Exmoor's characteristic red soil. Wildlife is abundant here, the famous red deer, well camouflaged against a background of russet-coloured autumn bracken, the pheasants in their beautiful red-brown plumage strutting purposefully across the roads, quite oblivious to the dangers of passing traffic, and the native wild ponies which roam the barren hillsides in all weathers are just some of Exmoor's delights. Exmoor abounds with beauty – and scenery of great diversity.

There are deep, almost gorgelike, valleys shrouded with trees of all descriptions – a splendid sight in autumn – an artist's dream, when the colours change from lush green to glorious shades of golden brown. The bleak open moorland in the very heart of Exmoor, more often than not enveloped in low cloud, adds its own hint of mystery. It is easy then to see how Exmoor has inspired so many tales of superstition and enigmatic folklore.

Exmoor was made a National Park in 1954 and despite its size, 265 square miles, the smallest National Park in Britain, it contains many differing landscapes – cornfields, dry heath, winding river valleys, marshland and high moor. The wide variety is probably due to the great range in altitude over a relatively small area, giving rise to local pockets of weather which govern the agricultural use of the land, as well as providing different habitats for wildlife. Some of the species of wild flowers and plants which you may find are the delicate sundew, which grows in wet boggy areas along with the bog asphodel, a plant poisonous to animals but none the less attractive with its orange-yellow flowers, and on the drier heathlands, shrubs such as gorse, bracken and whortleberries. These berries are considered quite a delicacy among Somerset folk, and in autumn the curious sight of people bent double scouring the undergrowth for enough fruit to make a whortleberry pie is a common occurrence.

Dunkery Beacon.

Stark, storm-lashed trees show the darker side of Exmoor's weather but have a strange compelling beauty of their own. Many of Exmoor's trees suffered in the storms of 1990 and some much-loved landmarks have gone for ever.

CURIOSITIES OF EXMOOR WEATHER

I N FEBRUARY 1990, the Westcountry, and most of Britain, suffered ferocious winds and storms which uprooted trees, causing damage to many buildings. Floods ruined houses and made farmland unworkable. Those living by the coast could only watch in horror as mountainous seas lashed sea defences, tossing rocks and debris about like bits of paper in the wind. People said they could not remember seeing such extreme conditions before. Just a year previously we had experienced the driest summer on record, and again the population was mystified as to the cause. The picture of Wimbleball reservoir shows just how dry that summer was, and it is no wonder we were on the brink of drought conditions. We may believe the 'greenhouse effect' is to blame but a newspaper cutting dated March 10 1891 proves that harsh weather was affecting the counties of Somerset, Devon and Cornwall just as savagely then.

This was the time of the Great Blizzard. Spring had arrived on Exmoor, the lambs were born, the flowers in bloom and springlike sunshine warmed the pastures, encouraging new growth. But then disaster struck. Snow 300ft deep piled into the combes, 200 lives were lost, 6,000 sheep and lambs died. Fierce winds uprooted 500,000 trees, at sea 50 ships were wrecked in storms which left untold damage and destruction in their wake.

Another freak of nature was responsible for the Lynmouth Flood disaster in 1952, when torrential rain caused the River Lyn to surge down the valley sweeping away part of the town, destroying whole houses and taking the lives of 34 people.

Our weather is awesome and unpredictable. When you stand at the

15

top of Dunkery Beacon and survey the vast expanse of the sea in one direction and moorland in the other, views stretching far away into the distance towards Devon and Cornwall, you realise that there must be a great force responsible for all of this; more powerful than man, stronger than anything that man can build. We are no match for Mother Nature, and we are strongly aware of this in the heart of Exmoor.

The man who suffers most at the hand of the ever-changing weather must be the farmer. This little ditty summarises the farmer's plight:

> 'The farmer will never be happy again
> He carries his heart in his boots,
> For either the rain is destroying his grain
> Or the drought is destroying his roots.
> In fact, if you meet this unfortunate man
> The conclusion is only too plain
> That nature is just an elaborate plan
> To annoy him again and again.'

This Westcountry rhyme has been attributed to Rudyard Kipling who supposedly wrote it whilst at school in Westward Ho! While this is uncertain, whoever the author, he obviously had sympathy with the hard-working farmer.

———————◆———————

Wimbleball Reservoir at the height of 1989's drought clearly demonstrates the seriousness of the water shortage in the Westcountry that summer.

HAUNTED EXMOOR

E XMOOR'S atmosphere can well be described as haunting.
Cornish author Michael Williams, a man who has been delving
into the supernatural for a quarter of a century, has both ridden and
walked across Exmoor. He says: 'I'm not surprised there have been so
many ghostly claims on Exmoor. The truth is that Exmoor has a very
strong sense of the past and, even today, in places, can seem remote as
the moon. There is, too, this wonderful beckoning quality on Exmoor,
luring you on and on beyond the next valley, over the next hill, and
never with unfulfilled promise.'

This sense of mystery and the supernatural is not merely an echo
from a distant past or secondhand experience, the impression contin-
ues to this very day. Fellow Bossiney author Peter Underwood,
President of the Ghost Club, who has been described as 'Britain's
Ghost Hunter Supreme' devoted a chapter in his *Mysterious Places* to
the strange goings-on at a farmhouse on the edge of Exmoor, where
mysterious voices were heard in the middle of the night and other
curious happenings took place.

Exmoor can boast a rich variety of hauntings – black dogs on the
moor, rattling chains, several sightings of sad figures with tragic pasts.
One such tale is of the farmer who drowned in Pinkworthy Pond, a
very lonely spot and even on a bright day appearing cold and depress-

*Looking towards the old ruined tower in the grounds of Lee Abbey – a
view that conveys Exmoor's haunting atmosphere.*

ing. The young man had thrown himself into the dark waters leaving behind him on the bank his hat and coat, the only clues to his fate. The pond was eventually drained to uncover the body lying close to the edge in shallow water. The ghost of this unfortunate man is said to haunt the pond and on a chilly grey winter's day, alone on the moor, who would dare to doubt the truth of this tale?

Porlock had its own ghost, a notorious character called Lucott, who only a week after his death was sighted in spirit form at Porlock Weir. He defied all attempts to exorcise him, mocking the holy men who had been sent for to rid the village of this troublesome nuisance. He even taunted them inside the church itself. Finally he met his match in one parson who boldly rode with him to Watchet then, enticing the ghost into a box, closed the lid and tossed it into the sea.

The Valley of Rocks where strange formations glimpsed in mist or semi-darkness can stir the imagination.

There are many curious tales told about hunting, of packs of ghost hounds, headless huntsmen and even stranger stories of witches who take on the form of an animal such as a hare or fox and lead the hunt a merry dance on a treacherous trail, only to revert to their human shape when faced with capture. Then there are accounts of unusual happenings, as on the day of the funeral of the hunt's most memorable Harbourer, when the mourners looked up from the graveside to see on the skyline several mature stags, their fine antlers clearly outlined.

They seemed to have come to bid farewell, or perhaps these were the spirits of stags who had suffered their fate at the hands of this hunt servant. Whether apparition or reality, the explanations are uncertain but this is not the only tale of a rare sighting of a number of fully grown stags gathered together. The deer appeared at another funeral, this time that of a renowned huntsman, almost as though they knew an adversary had passed away and they had come to pay their respects or perhaps stand and watch his departure with relief.

There are several old houses and farms within Exmoor's bounds which provide us with colourful tales of ghostly sightings and strange occurrences. Combe Sydenham is an Elizabethan manor which holds more than one mystery within its walls. A cavalier wearing a cloak and Spanish hat presented himself at the bedside of an unsuspecting guest one night, and a portrait of Major Sydenham was reputed to have strange qualities. The eyes of the figure in the picture were said to follow people around the room. The Sydenham coach is supposed to haunt the grounds, drawn by six or eight horses shod with silver.

AROUND PORLOCK

PORLOCK is a delightfully unspoilt village despite the fact that it
sees hundreds of tourists each year. I wonder if these visitors are
aware that they are following in the footsteps of the poet Southey who,
on being caught in a shower of rain, sheltered in the old Ship Inn and
penned this sonnet in recollection of his visit:-

> 'Porlock! I shall forget thee not,
> Here by the unwelcome summer rain confined;
> But often shall hereafter call to mind
> How here, a patient prisoner, 'twas my lot
> To wear the lonely, lingering close of day,
> Making my sonnet by the alehouse fire,
> Whilst Idleness and Solitude inspire
> Dull rhymes to pass the duller hours away.'

A chimney-corner at the inn is said to have been Southey's favourite
seat.

The church at Porlock, with its truncated spire, the octagonal sides
faceted with oak shingles, has many features that capture the imagination. It is believed to date back to the thirteenth century when it was
built on the original site of a Saxon church. Inside are the carved figures of one of Henry V's knights of Agincourt and his wife. Both are
finely dressed, he in full armour, hands clasped over his badge and his
lady in rich clothing, her mitred head-dress embellished with lace displaying the royal fleur-de-lys, together creating a splendid monument
to the age of chivalry.

The tower of St. Dubricius.

Porlock church has also been the subject of one of Somerset's most notorious prophets, old Mother Shipton. According to her prophecy, 'When ships use the spire of Porlock's St. Dubricius as a mooring, then Exmoor will have vanished beneath the waves!' Porlock village itself appears to have been a place of some importance long ago in Saxon times, probably at about the time of the building of its original church, when princes and lords hunted not only Exmoor's famous red deer but also the wild boar which roamed in the forest. The 'port' of Porlock is known to have been the landing site for several unsuccessful attempts to invade Somerset. The sea has now receded and left a flat plain of fertile farmland, and the tiny harbour of Porlock Weir is almost a mile away from the original land-locked port.

All along the north coast of Devon and Somerset, in the sixth and seventh centuries, invasions of a different kind took place. The Celtic missionaries began their infiltration, coming into Exmoor from Wales and Ireland. This explains why so many of the churches are dedicated to Celtic saints with curious names such as St. Dubricius, who suppos-

A team of sturdy horses ready to set off with a coach-load of smartly dressed passengers from the Ship Inn, Porlock.

edly crowned King Arthur, St. Decuman, St. Beuno, St. Petroc and St. Carantoc who were all Welsh and St. Brendan who was Irish.

Proof of the coming of the missionaries exists in Culbone Church 'the smallest complete parish church in England' of which St. Beuno, born in Powys in the sixth century, is the patron saint. Culbone, hidden deep in the combe, reached only by a rough track, is a little gem which according to Arthur Mee in his book 'Somerset', 'clings like a wren's nest, to the wooded cliffs'. Culbone means the cell of Beuno, but was once called 'Kitnor' meaning the cave by the shore. It would be an ideal sanctuary, a retreat when the hectic pace of life became too much to bear. In fact its remoteness suggests that this is what it was intended to be, an oasis in the midst of a troubled land. Despite the difficult access to this 'Tiny Temple' it is well attended every Sunday by parishioners who brave all weathers. On a warm sunny day in summer many a visitor to the area may be enticed to travel the rocky path to have the privilege of worshipping in such a unique little house of God.

Buried in dense woodland near Culbone church lies a curious stone which bears a carving of a wheeled cross. This stone near the ancient ridgeway from Lynmouth to Porlock is believed to have been part of a stone row separated to act as a signpost to Culbone church. The old road, now roughly followed by the A39, passed through the earthworks on Wind Hill and by the barrows on Kipscombe, Cosgate and Culbone Hills, skirting just south of the carved cross. There is much evidence of early Bronze Age settlement on Exmoor and the ancient routes marked by the standing stones, various barrows and cairns scattered over the moor are still well defined to this day. Records show that medieval bounds of Exmoor trace part of one particular track and some parish boundaries follow another; in fact as they criss-cross the bleak moorland separating the counties of Devon and Somerset it is curious to think people, who inhabited Exmoor as long ago as 2000 BC, could have left such a lasting impression on the landscape – their lines of communication still in use in the twentieth century.

It is rare to see a cyclist, in North Devon and Exmoor actually mounted on his machine. The hills are so incredibly steep and long that it would take great strength and stamina, not to mention sheer courage, to cycle either up or down them. At the top of daunting

Porlock Hill, which strikes fear into the hearts of many a cautious motorist, let alone a cyclist, is a sign which reads 'CYCLISTS ARE ADVISED TO WALK!'

This advice is well worth taking. The road drops sharply in a gradient of 1:4, twisting and winding through the trees until it levels out on reaching the village of Porlock below. There are many other hills besides Porlock notorious for their steepness: Countisbury, 25 per cent or 1:4; Lynmouth, also 25 per cent but much shorter, and another, well known as a test hill in motor trials, Beggar's Roost. This is now only a by-road but is still frequently used for trials such as the 'Land's End', tackled at night by cars and motorcycles, offering a challenge to the enthusiasts who participate in these gruelling events.

The coaches which plied between Porlock and Lynmouth carrying tourists and day trippers were given names relating to Exmoor, such as Lorna Doone and Red Deer. They were generally a coach and four but to tackle the steeper hills such as Countisbury, an extra pair was added to help climb the gradient. When the coaches became motorised the names were transferred to the modern counterparts. They met with many adventures on their travels and looking through old photographs it is easy to pick out the familiar face of a driver who must have covered hundreds of miles in his time as a coachman, appearing over and over again in pictures taken in different places along the northern part of Exmoor.

◆

The 'little gem' of Culbone Church.

THE EXMOOR PONY

WINTER on Exmoor is a time of extreme hardship. The climate is cold and wet, often with thick snow covering much of the moors. The animals who live there have to be hardy and capable of surviving without extra food from man. The Exmoor pony is one of the best 'survivors', it has been called 'The Child of the Moor', gradually moulded by harsh weather and bleak living conditions into the delightfully tough little character we see roaming wild on Exmoor today.

Classed as a rare breed because of the small numbers in existence, the Exmoor pony can rightfully claim to be Britain's oldest pony with a history which can be traced back millions of years to the Ice Age. Fossil bones have been discovered and compared with those of the modern pony. There is a clear resemblance between the jawbone of the ponies who once roamed the tundra-like conditions of the British Isles during the Ice Age and the Exmoor pony as we know it today. Many rare breeds of cattle and sheep have increased in number over the past years, but despite the efforts of the Rare Breeds Trust and the Exmoor Pony Society the number of Exmoor ponies has remained static.

The Exmoor Pony Society was formed in 1921 with the aim of establishing herds and improving the breeding of the true Exmoor pony and this it has done with great success though problems have arisen with the limited number of bloodlines.

Records of the ponies can be seen in the Domesday Book and one of the earliest recognised herds, the Anchor Herd, so called because of the anchor shaped brand, was first recorded in 1818. The herd was

Exmoor ponies at home in their moorland world of summer plenty – but harsher times can follow.

owned by Sir Thomas Dyke Acland of Holnicott, an early master of staghounds, who held the last lease of Exmoor from the Crown which expired in 1814. The land was then offered for sale and bought almost entirely by Mr John Knight, who was responsible for the 'reclamation' of the moors. Descendants of Acland's herd can still be seen on Winsford Hill carrying the Anchor mark.

In 1957 Herd 1 was established based on the Anchor Herd and other herds have since stemmed from this. The ponies themselves are full of character with their distinctive 'mealy' muzzle, toad eye, short pricked ears, black points and primitive dun, brown or bay colouring. They are somewhat small in stature but extremely strong and equally at home under saddle or in harness. They are very tough and can roam wild on the moor all year round, the only link between them and human beings being the statutory brand mark on the flank, by which they can be identified when the herds are rounded up and brought down to the farms in autumn. The 'suckers' as the foals are called, can then be registered and branded.

It is a stirring sight to see a herd of ponies being driven along the narrow winding lanes leading down from the moors, running wild and free with their young at their heels. They have reared them unaided on the unforgiving moor, usually under the watchful eye of their owners but without interference, maintaining the independence and inbred hardiness of the genuine moorland pony.

DULVERTON

O N THE road between Dulverton and Bampton is a spot which is reputedly haunted. Chains have been heard rattling at night and local people have long thought that the devil presides over this place.

A curious little tale was told by a man from Bampton back in the days when the boneshaker bicycle was something of a novelty. Apparently a member of a well-known household in the area was riding down the hill in the twilight on his machine which was rattling and creaking merrily, when halfway down he encountered a farm labourer who had never seen such a thing in his life before. Meeting this apparition in the 'dimpsey' (half-light) made the poor man immediately jump to the conclusion that this was an apparition and in terror he turned and fled. Whatever the explanation, folks agree this stretch of road at night differs from any other in being distinctly 'uncanny'.

Dulverton is a bustling town within the southern boundary of the Exmoor National Park. It is very old, with many quaint narrow streets, but the increase of traffic has led to the roads being widened and some of the ancient cottages being demolished. Beneath the rubble of one house an old coin was discovered which, according to one resident was a Spanish coin left by the Dons in 1600 when they invaded England. His companion disagreed wholeheartedly and said England had never been invaded by Spaniards, but the 'expert' insisted he 'knowed they did and it weren't likely they could pass Dulverton without stopping for a drink!' The coin turned out to be a sixpenny piece struck in 1566 and a poor specimen at that, but the story shows how Dulverton was in the past a popular meeting place for farmers and moorland folk.

Today it is a renowned centre for hunting and fishing. The hotels in

Above: *A peaceful uncluttered Dulverton in summer.*
Below: *Pixton Park, Dulverton, the beautiful home of the Waugh family – now divided into flats.*

33

Dulverton before the fire of 1916 which destroyed some of the pretty cottages.

the vicinity cater for those visitors who come to Exmoor to take part in outdoor pursuits, providing permits for anglers wanting to fish the well-stocked rivers for salmon or trout, packed lunches for keen hikers and even stabling for the horses of itinerate hunters. There are plenty of activities to choose from, pony trekking is popular and riders can

Dulverton after the fire. The fire appliance would have come from what is now the Town Hall.

enjoy the scenery of Exmoor, reaching places inaccessible by car. For the walker, the footpaths (some 600 miles in all) are clearly marked, with coloured signs painted on gateposts, trees and stones to point the way.

During the hunting season, the middle of August to the end of April, Dulverton sees many keen sportsmen and women assemble from all over the country. They come to follow the two packs of staghounds, the Devon & Somerset, whose kennels are at Exford, and the Tiverton. The Exmoor Foxhounds have their kennels at Simonsbath, their hunting country covers much of the moor stretching from

Horse and rider traverse the ford in Bury village.

Bratton Fleming in the west to Wheddon Cross in the east. It is a pack with a fine reputation and the remote, largely unspoilt countryside is the envy of many other packs. Hunting, whether for foxes, deer or hare is an emotive subject but, without condemning it or condoning it, it is impossible to write about Exmoor and not mention 'the chase'. For many country people who dwell on the moor it is not a sport, it is a way of life. For generations the hunting traditions have been kept alive and the sight of huntsman and hounds on Exmoor is probably one of the few things that has remained virtually unchanged over the centuries.

———————◆———————

Wood carver Septimus Waugh who carved the first St. George and the dragon since the Renaissance. It has been donated to Dulverton Church.

An impression of author R.D. Blackmore by artist Felicity Young.

R.D. BLACKMORE

NO BOOK on Exmoor would be complete without mentioning the man who in his novel *Lorna Doone* brought together so many of the Moor's legends and superstitions, producing a whole new interest in the area by visitors hot on the trail of the notorious Doones, speculating as to where they lived, looking for Lorna's Bower or the waterslide referred to in the story.

How curious then that a man so bound up with Exmoor was born in Berkshire and lived a great part of his life in Teddington, Middlesex. Richard Doddridge Blackmore was born in 1825, from North Devon stock. Most of his boyhood experiences were confined almost entirely to this county. His greatest achievement in literature was inspired by Westcountry legend, some would perhaps think Devon legend, but a large part of Exmoor is actually in Somerset. Lorna Doone can be considered as a 'border' romance, Badgeworthy Water, the site of the Doone Valley, actually forms part of the county boundary. Much contention existed about the exact location of Blackmore's Doone Valley, but the Ordnance Survey Director has now officially said that the Badgeworthy Water which runs through Lankcombe is the correct siting and not the neighbouring valley of Hoccombe.

Lankcombe provides us with the famous waterslide and an open gateway which some guide books call 'Doone Gate' though it is quite likely that Blackmore created his valley out of many features in the area and brought them together as 'The Doone Valley'. It may just be sheer chance that Badgeworthy Water neatly fits the description.

Blackmore had a grandfather, the Reverend John Blackmore, who was rector of Oare. They spent much time together, and probably the

Oare Church, little changed since the young R.D. Blackmore attended services there while staying with his grandfather.

Reverend John recounted many tales of local folklore and history. This may be where young Richard first heard the story of Lorna Doone for it was well known in North Devon long before it became a literary success for the adult author R.D. Blackmore. The family pedigree stretches back much further in its connection with North Devon than the Reverend John. The parish register at Parracombe shows this and the Blackmore family initials of J.B. and R.B. 1638 can be seen over the porch of the old farmhouse at Parracombe. R.D. Blackmore was later sent to live with his uncle Richard at the moorland village of Charles, in the Bray Valley, where it is said he wrote much of his novel. His uncle was Rector there and Charles Parsonage was where the famous romantic tale was finally penned. Throughout his boyhood Blackmore gleaned stories of interest, legend and superstition to use in the book. One of the most curious tales was that of Tom Faggus and his 'Enchanted Strawberry Horse'.

According to folklore, Tom Faggus was a debonair highwayman, a blacksmith from North Molton, 'a rough rude place on the edge of Exmoor, as Blackmore described it. Left destitute by a law suit he turned to crime, becoming a gentleman robber, collecting 'contributions' from travellers on the highway, only robbing the rich, sparing the poor or sick. On one occasion a group of farmers gathered together to ride home from Barnstaple fair, believing safety in numbers would protect them from the attentions of Tom Faggus. But luck was not on their side. As they reached the post at Bratton Down Faggus appeared, brandishing a pistol in each hand and mounted astride the strawberry mare Winnie. The farmers, under threat of death, deposited their money at the foot of the post watching in silence as Faggus galloped off in triumph with his haul.

Later he was seized at Simonsbath, but he whistled to his faithful horse who broke down the stable door and rushed to the aid of her master. She galloped into the alehouse where Faggus was being held and, with hooves flying, carried him away. Believing he was safe he was dismayed to encounter parties of men at Barnstaple Bridge blocking his path. Seeing no other means of escape Faggus put his horse at the parapet of the bridge and clearing it, swam away to safety.

There was no end to Faggus' cunning in trying to part people from their money. One day news was received at Exford that Faggus would pass through the village. The men waited to ambush him but he fooled them by approaching in disguise and even volunteering to join them in their attempt to capture the notorious villain. He suggested they fire their pistols to make sure they were in good working order and while their guns were unloaded he drew his own, declared his name and made off with the loot. His 'enchanted' horse saved him on several occasions, helping him escape from angry crowds, leaving in his wake bewildered and dumbfounded victims.

Faggus was finally tricked by an officer disguised as an old beggar-woman at the inn at Exbridge. He called for his horse but in vain because the unfortunate animal had been cruelly shot. Faggus was hoisted, by a rope fastened around his feet, to the ceiling and all was over for the celebrated robber. Accounts differ as to what happened after his capture. Some say he was tried at Taunton Assizes and later hanged, though no record of this has ever been found. Others say he was pardoned and released. In all his escapades he performed not one single act of cruelty or violence. Rather like the legendary Robin Hood, he stole from the rich to give to the poor.

———————◆———————

The beautiful interior of Oare Church – its sense of history may well have helped form R.D. Blackmore's wish to immortalise in print some of his grandfather's local tales.

LORNA DOONE STATUE

THE ENCHANTING bronze sculpture seen opposite gives us an impression of what Lorna Doone may have looked like. Her dress is an accurate reproduction of 17th century attire; the Victoria and Albert Museum was consulted and their advice taken on this important detail. The statue was sculpted by George Stephenson of Exeter, commissioned by the late Dr. Whitman Pearson of New Hampshire U.S.A, who was president of the Anglo-American Lorna Doone Society.

This sculpture is a symbol, representing the common interest shown in Britain and across the Atlantic, in the timeless romantic tale of *Lorna Doone*. It has captured the hearts of many and inspires hundreds of visitors to come to 'Doone Country' every year. They come to experience the breathtaking scenery of this special part of Exmoor and to imagine themselves back in the time of the Doones, soaking up the atmosphere of the locations R.D. Blackmore chose for the setting of his novel.

The sculpture is presently with the English representative of the society, Barry Gardner who is a well known artist. The intention is to place the statue in the grounds of Exmoor House in Dulverton, the headquarters of the Exmoor National Park. The unveiling of the statue will coincide with the launch of a sequel to R.D. Blackmore's *Lorna Doone*, entitled *Doone Ransom* written by Barry Gardner.

AROUND WINSFORD

A CURIOUS legend surrounds Tarr Steps, one of England's finest old bridges. Its origin uncertain, it may be medieval or even date back to the Bronze Age, but ask almost any local person and they will recount the 'true' story behind Tarr Steps. The bridge, built of large unhewn stone slabs laid across low piers standing about two or three feet above the River Barle, was placed there, it was said, by the Devil who menaced any mortal soul who dared disturb him whilst he sunbathed on the stones.

On one occasion, the Devil took his seat on one side and a fearless parson occupied the other, eager to do battle with the Prince of Darkness. The holy man was very wily, he first sent a cat across the Steps, and on reaching the other bank the poor creature was torn to pieces. This served to break the spell and the parson strode boldly across the bridge to challenge the Devil to a conflict of words. The Devil was sure he would have the advantage but the parson uttered such abuse that, taken aback, the enemy of mankind was forced to retire, vanquished. From then on travellers could pass freely over the bridge.

This particular part of Exmoor, around Winsford, is shrouded in superstition. The Wambarrows, the highest point on Winsford Hill at Comer's Gate, are three fine examples of Bronze Age burial mounds, supposedly haunted by a strange black dog. Mounsey Castle, the remains of one of several Iron Age hill forts in the area is apparently the scene of chariot races at midnight which circle the castle and then vanish mysteriously into a cairn in a nearby field at the foot of the hill. Another curious relic, dating back to the Dark Ages, is the menhir, the

WINSFORD

The timelessness of an Exmoor village is reflected in the calm waters below this little bridge at Winsford.

Opposite: Everyone's idea of a country pub – the Royal Oak at Winsford.

Caratacus Stone also on Winsford Hill. Its inscription reads CARAT-ACI NEPUS, meaning kinsman of Caratacus, possibly a marker for the burial place of a 'Romanised' British Chieftain, and dates from between the fifth to the seventh century A.D.

Records show it to have been in its present position since at least 1219 but historians and archaeologists are baffled as to why this curious stone with its partially obliterated and crude inscription, was placed facing the valley to the north east and away from the dominating ridge of Winsford Hill. They agree though that the stone belongs to a time when the inhabitants of Britain were battling with the Roman invaders. In 1936 the stone was uprooted and left lying on its side. Experts were alarmed. The stone had remained untouched for years, apart from a scratch caused by a runaway cart and a scar where a farm labourer had supposedly hewn a chunk of rock out of it in the nineteenth century. Who had done this and why?

Some believed it was thieves in search of treasure, which according to local legend lies buried beneath the stone. Folk told of a wagon and horses heard crossing the moors that night, supposedly carrying the plunder. But as few people were brave enough to venture out on Exmoor, renowned for its after dark hauntings the true story can never be known.

Winsford is a pretty little village nestling deep in one of Exmoor's delightful valleys. Here the Winn Brook joins the River Exe. Just as several roads converge to create the heart of the village so do the waters, flowing down from the moor, meet to give rise to Winsford's most delightful feature, its eight bridges. The pack-horse bridge and ford are a common feature of the picturesque villages on Exmoor. Of the eight bridges, three span the larger River Exe; the Exe pack-horse bridge is very old and at one time the only route to the Brendon Hills. It is hard to imagine, in these days of lorries and other goods vehicles, that at one time everything had to be carried to and from the moors by pack-horse.

There are other interesting things to see in Winsford. The cottages themselves have stories to tell. On the road which leads to Dulverton, opposite the Post Office, is the cottage where famous statesman, wartime Minister of Labour and Foreign Secretary Ernest Bevin was born on March 7 1881. He lived in this small cottage for part of his childhood, the youngest of seven children, but his early years were not happy ones. His mother never revealed his father's identity, the father of the other six children had mysteriously disappeared while the family was away from Winsford, long before Ernest was born. When he was only eight years old his mother, whom he loved dearly, became ill and died, leaving him a wretched orphan.

He moved away from the Somerset village to live in Devon. His tough childhood was obviously good grounding for his future career in politics. He went on to become a well respected figure both in Britain and internationally. The people of Winsford will always remember this Somerset boy made good – the plaque on the wall of the cottage serves as a memorial to a great man.

One of the most attractive buildings in the village is the Royal Oak, with its thatched roof, low ceilings and its sign, in keeping with the tradition of ancient inns, hanging from its own post. One of the most photographed inns in all of the Westcountry, it is full of old-fashioned charm and draws in the visitors like a magnet.

Ernest Bevin's birthplace.

TARR STEPS

More than one way to cross the water at Tarr Steps – a rider and his mount skilfully negotiate the river....

....and two spaniels scorn the easy way across the stones, preferring a cool, refreshing swim.

WILDLIFE AND THE RED DEER

VIEWING Exmoor from the comfort of a car is possible – but not recommended. To experience the atmosphere you should leave your vehicle and walk along one of the many trackways criss-crossing the open moorland. You will need your wellingtons as much of the area is boggy and wet underfoot, but this moor is a paradise for the botanist with so many species of wild flowers to be found. There are also drier areas of heathland, areas with peaty soils and rocky river valleys – each has its own special flowers.

Wildlife, both bird and animal, can be spotted on the high moorland. Buzzards are a common sight now though at one time their numbers were on the decline; there is a great variety of other hawks too, merlin, sparrowhawk and kestrel, living off rabbits, mice, voles and even snakes which lurk in the undergrowth. Grouse, snipe, wheatear, whinchat and stonechat are quite common on the moorland plateau, and the dipper can be seen bobbing and diving in the streams. Many birds use Exmoor as a wintering ground, including fieldfare, redwing, the short-eared owl and the hen harrier. The list, it seems, is endless and hours of watching are well rewarded by a glimpse of one of these beautiful birds.

The most thrilling wildlife sight for many must be the red deer. Red deer have not always been as abundant as today. In the reign of James I there were no red deer in the forest. Numbers increased with the careful management of the Aclands in the 1700s but following the sale of the only pack of staghounds in 1825 the numbers again declined and poaching was common. It was clear better husbandry was necessary to prevent the deer becoming extinct on Exmoor. In 1825 after

their numbers dwindled to only a handful, Mr John Knight began the task of preserving what deer were left. Gradually they became more plentiful and other landowners contributed to their preservation by containing them within their estates, setting up special reserves. One such area was Oare Common which after being enclosed in 1860 exclusively for the deer became known as the Deer Park.

The red deer stands, with his antlers, some six feet tall, Britain's biggest wild animal. There can be no finer sight than that of a mature stag with a magnificent pair of antlers standing amidst the autumn bracken, his red coat blending with his surroundings or proudly silhouetted against the horizon, reminding us of Landseer's famous portrait The Monarch of the Glen. It is one of nature's most majestic creatures.

The deer cast their antlers every year, but these prized relics are hard to find as the shedding takes places in the deepest thickets and is rarely witnessed. There is a specific way of describing a stag's head. For example a stag who is said to have 'all his rights, with three and four atop' carries two large sweeping, curved beams, and from each of these project three long points. Starting at the base they are the brow, the bay and the trey. Above these are seven further points issuing upwards from the beams, three on one, and four on the other, making the animal a 'thirteen pointer'. The stag's head does not necessarily tell his age, but a young immature stag, or 'pricket', is easily recognised by the short stumps on either side of his brow from which grow thin 'spires'. As he gets older the brow rights appear then in successive years the bay and trey are added and so on, until he has a full head. The most number of points ever recorded is an amazing twenty points. The head increases in size with age and the spread between the beams can reach up to three feet.

The Exmoor stag casts his antlers by the end of April, the new growth begins to appear but is covered in 'velvet'. The deer are often seen helpless against the summer flies which swarm around the newly forming antlers, standing head down trying to keep as still as possible for fear of knocking the velvet which is extremely sensitive and bleeds easily if torn. Once the head is formed then the velvet dries and by August or September the stags are to be found rubbing vigorously against the trees to remove every last trace. The magnificent antlers which a stag carries are not merely for show, they also make formidable weapons against rivals, the brow points being especially dangerous when the stag is engaged in serious fighting during the rutting season. The deer are well camouflaged in the Exmoor undergrowth, the ruddy-brown coat blends in with the bracken and typical red soil, the antlers looking like tree branches when the creatures freeze when danger threatens. To study deer is fascinating and not as difficult as some may imagine. It needs patience and determination, but these are well rewarded when at last a herd is sighted and observed in its natural habitat.

The deer have exerted a strong influence over the land and the people of Exmoor, they have been the subject of paintings by well-known artists such as Lionel Edwards, famous for his sporting scenes, and they have been written about in poetry and in stories. Henry Williamson wrote a collection of tales under the title *The Old Stag* and Richard Jefferies wrote *Red Deer* in 1883.

You are constantly reminded of their presence – the road sign warning motorists to beware of deer on the road – the Exmoor National Park emblem which appears on signs and souvenirs as a fitting trade mark and the houses, farms and inns which have been named after them. One erstwhile hostelry called Red Deer was situated on the road between Exford and Simonsbath and became known locally as 'Gallon House' because the beer was always sold by the gallon, a normal measure for the miners who were mining the iron ore in the area at that time. Gallon House is mentioned in *Lorna Doone*, and though actually called Red Deer, R.D. Blackmore must have been acquainted with its local name as he refers to a 'gallon of ale' being drunk at a public house near Exford.

Another animal which features strongly in the Exmoor way of life is the horse, not only the wild pony of the moor but the domesticated variety. Many houses have a horse peering out over a stable door, the sight of the village blacksmith toiling away is no rarity and in every lane there is the chance you will meet a horse and rider enjoying the scenery, for what better way can there be to see Exmoor than from the saddle?

'What better way can there be to see Exmoor than from the saddle?'....above: *a group of riders plods steadily across the moor near Dunkery and,* opposite: *a photograph that encapsulates the essential Exmoor as horse and rider go through the water at Malmsmead.*

'WE'LL LAUNCH FROM PORLOCK'

TO HEAR a story of courage and endeavour about the crew of a lifeboat is not unusual. This rare breed of men often put their lives at risk to save seamen in trouble in the treacherous waters around the British Isles. But the rescue of the crew and three-masted ship the 'Forest Hall' on the night of January 12 1899 is a unique tale. The bravery of the men involved deserves recognition and the events of that night will remain in the annals of the village of Lynmouth for years to come. The cruel sea off the Exmouth coastline has claimed its fair share of victims and the Bristol Channel is littered with uncharted wrecks which are now popular fishing grounds. Conger, skate, pollock, cod, bass and tope are a few of the varieties of fish which inhabit the waters off shore making sea angling a prolific pastime. The wrecks beneath the waves can harbour curious secrets. Occasionally we get a glimpse of the past. In a secret location one vessel, in certain weather conditions, belches oil fumes which bubble to the surface from the depths. Her identity unknown, she lies as a reminder of the war, still laden with her cargo. Many other ships have foundered on the rocks below the towering cliffs, adding to the loss of life in this small area. But for the men of Lynmouth and the lifeboat crew that toll would certainly have been higher. Their daring exploits on that January night when 100 men and 20 horses hauled the lifeboat 'Louisa' up the notorious Countisbury Hill, and down fearsome Porlock Hill, to launch the boat at Porlock during one of the worst storms in living memory almost defy description.

What drives men to perform such an incredible feat? It seems the men of Lynmouth were bound together by a strange spirit, a spirit which united the community. The sea had dominated their lives for generations, and the whole village had an inherent sense of duty towards any mortal soul in peril on the ocean.

Lynmouth's spirit was shown again on August 15 1952, when millions of tons of floodwater poured down the valley leaving death and destruction in its wake. Lynmouth had been transformed from a bustling tourist attraction packed with visitors, to a place of utter devastation. Despite the magnitude of the disaster, within hours a meeting had been called and the people of Lynmouth were already making plans to rebuild the community. Such was the strength of will to overcome tragedy and piece together the shattered lives of those worst affected.

The lifeboat Louisa which made the epic journey.

In 1899 the lifeboat men did not stop for one moment to consider whether carrying a lifeboat 15 miles, along a tortuous route, made sense. Nor did they feel heroic, it was their duty. As it happened the journey was not strictly necessary. The messages which passed between coastguard, ship and lifeboat signalman were confused. The 'Forest Hall' had been passed a line by the tug 'Jollife' and was not hopelessly adrift as reported. But the brave men of Lynmouth thought there were lives in danger. The crew agreed the only way to launch the 'Louisa' was to take her overland to Porlock, commandeering as many horses as the local stable could supply. These horses were used to the journey, they regularly pulled the coaches between the villages but they had never all been harnessed together at one time.

A team of horses hauls a coach up notorious Countisbury Hill.

What a sight it must have been, 20 horses, 100 men, the lifeboat on its carriage, lanterns glowing and flickering in the wind and the relentless rain lashing down as they crossed the Lyndale Bridge. It is a mystery how they managed to climb to the top of Countisbury Hill without disaster befalling them. If the weight of the carriage had caused it to run backwards it would have wreaked havoc among horses and men, but somehow they reached the summit without mishap. They cheered, but the victory was followed immediately by disappointment. As they came out onto the bleak storm-lashed moor they reached a spot called Ashton Gate. Here the track was too narrow for their load. Someone came up with a bright idea – the lifeboat had a set of skids, used for launching her on sandy beaches, they could be used to guide her round the gate and over the moorland until the track widened. The skids were duly placed under her and she was hauled painfully along, the skids having to be moved each time she inched forward.

At last, exhausted and soaked to the skin, they spotted the lights in the cottage windows far below in Porlock village but the horror of the night was yet to come, the descent of Porlock Hill. The horses were unhitched and kept at a safe distance as to overrun them on the hill would have caused serious injury. They reached the last bend on the terrible twisting hill, only to be confronted by the wall of a cottage. With no other way round they decided to knock it down, with the startled permission of its owner. She watched, dumbfounded by the sight of a lifeboat outside her window, as rain-soaked men hacked down her wall with axes.

The 'Louisa' was finally launched at 8 am, having had to detour around the back of Porlock church before reaching the beach. How they had the strength to row through gale-force winds and storm-tossed seas to reach the 'Forest Hall' no-one will ever know, but they managed it, weary and somewhat bewildered by what they found when they arrived. The ship was helpless with her rudder smashed, but she had got both anchors down and out of the gloom appeared the tug 'Joliffe' which had been standing by all night. The danger which the Lynmouth men had feared no longer existed.

It was decided to tow the 'Forest Hall' into Barry as the seas off Lynmouth were still too dangerous to navigate. The lifeboat crew was so exhausted that half were put aboard the 'Forest Hall' while the others remained on the 'Louisa', escorting the stricken ship safely to harbour. Hours after leaving Lynmouth in such dramatic circumstances the lifeboat returned to her home port though not to a hero's welcome. The crew had done its duty and expected no reward or recognition. They did, in fact, each receive an extra £5, in those days a good sum of money, but they had to pay for repairs to the demolished cottage wall. This would have left them well out of pocket had not the grateful owners of the 'Forest Hall' contributed some £75.

Lynmouth from the Sea.

INSPIRATION

E XMOOR has for centuries inspired writers and painters, not just those who depict the moor itself but providing an atmosphere allowing great writers and poets to produce memorable works which have become classics.

Exmoor's most famous author must be R.D. Blackmore, who warrants a special chapter in this book. His is the distinction of drawing the attention of a wide number of readers to the existence of Exmoor through his tale of romance and family feud, *Lorna Doone*. For many visitors to Exmoor the Doones are the prime reason for coming, to identify parts of the moor with places in the book, to follow the 'Doone trail', but he has served to open everyone's eyes to the beauty of the moor.

Besides R.D. Blackmore, Exmoor's hall of fame holds such literary figures as Robert Southey, Poet Laureate, who lodged at Minehead in 1799, Shelley, Wordsworth and Coleridge. It was whilst staying at a farmhouse near Culbone, that Coleridge is believed to have dreamt the incidents in his unfinished poem *Kubla Khan* – unfinished because he was interrupted by a 'man from Porlock' who broke his train of thought and the fragments of the dream were lost forever. Coleridge on several occasions walked along the coast between Watchet and Lynton, enjoying the scenery with his friends the Wordsworths. It was on one of these walks that they discussed Coleridge's epic poem *The Rime of the Ancient Mariner.*

Henry Williamson, well known for his delightful tale *Tarka the Otter*, must have been inspired by the beauty of Exmoor and its wildlife. He wrote numerous stories about Exmoor's red deer as did many other

George Peppin who left Exmoor for Australia and, below: the tough handsome sheep he bred, the Peppin Merino, still found today in New Zealand and South Africa as well as Australia.

authors and nature lovers before him. Dr Charles Collyns wrote *Chase of the Wild Red Deer* in 1862 and it has since become a classic. Richard Jefferies and Sir John Fortescue were each responsible for books about the deer and their life on Exmoor, and there have been several publications about other aspects of Exmoor's wildlife. Many evocative writings have come from the pens of Exmoor – inspired authors who obviously found themselves very much in tune with the natural beauty of the wild moorland. Some delightful poetry has been composed, capturing Exmoor's mood and atmosphere not only in the past, as in Henry Newbolt's *Song of Exmoor* – for many probably the best poem ever written about Exmoor – but also more recently for Exmoor still holds fascination and inspiration.

Artists cannot fail to pick up their brush and paint when faced with such glorious colour, ever-changing light and cloud formations which cry out to be transferred to canvas. Every shade of brown, the variations of red, green and gold, and the intense blue turning to cold grey are all there waiting for the artist. Several well known painters have delighted in the Exmoor scenery, Lionel Edwards spent a great deal of time studying the seasons. He produced outstanding sketches and paintings of the red deer in their natural surroundings, sympathetic illustration of their life throughout the year and paintings of the chase for which he was renowned. Another famous sporting artist who found inspiration on Exmoor was Sir Alfred Munnings, he spent much time in Horner woods watching the deer and painting amidst the glorious autumn-tinged slopes of this idyllic valley.

Exmoor is to the poet or painter a source of endless stimulation to the creative mind or eye. Its distinctive atmosphere, changeable moods and the beauty in its wildness will, for centuries to come, attract the artist and the writer to its very heart.

One particularly 'curious' character who lived on Exmoor was George Peppin. In 1850 he left his home in Old Shute, near Dulverton to make a better life for himself in Australia. He had been a sheep farmer, living a hard life on the unrelenting moorland, and he intended to continue this 'down under'. He had not bargained for the even harsher conditions which he faced when trying to rear sheep in the outback and soon he was a desperate man, struggling to survive. Eventually he applied himself to breeding a sheep capable of with-

The Australian tombstone that commemorates a brave Exmoor man.

standing such extreme conditions.

The Peppin Merino was the product of his careful selective breeding and it is still popular in New Zealand and South Africa as well as Australia. George Peppin in his diaries on days when he was up against his worst problems, wrote: 'Opened a case of gin'!

DUNSTER

A S YOU drive along the road towards Williton the landscape immediately strikes you as a sharp contrast to the steep hills just left behind at Porlock and Countisbury.

During the Middle Ages the little town of Dunster was a thriving seaport, but the waters have receded to leave this charming example of a medieval settlement high and dry well away from the coast. Dunster is situated beside the River Avill which descends from its source high up on Dunkery Hill right in the heart of the moor and flows out into the Bristol Channel. The course it follows is through a beautiful wooded valley, like a giant corridor of trees, and between the rolling hillsides, the very epitome of the Somerset landscape. On nearing Dunster the river passes between two hills, Gallox Hill to the east, and Grabbist Hill to the west. The path which walkers can take to reach Grabbist is curiously called Goosey Path, once Goost Weekes Path, named, so the story goes, because of its width, just enough to allow single file pedestrians who have to copy the farmyard geese and walk in procession. The hill was once the site of a medieval vineyard though the terraces can no longer easily be distinguished. There is however a curious depression on the side of the hill known as the Giant's Chair, where it is said that a giant sat to bathe his feet in the River Avill below and reached over to Dunster Castle for a towel.

Dunster, at the gate of Exmoor is the finest medieval village in the Westcountry, its antiquity obvious at every turn. The castle, perched high on a tor, rising like a sentinel above the houses, dates back to the Norman Conquest, though all trace of the original Norman keep has vanished as it was destroyed by order of Parliament in 1650. In all its

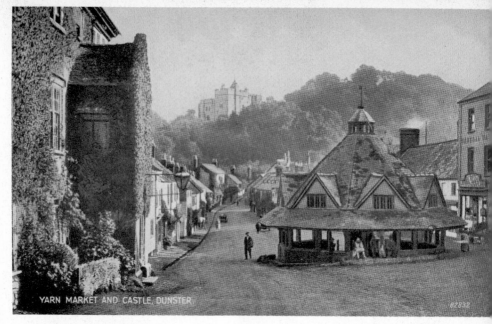

YARN MARKET AND CASTLE, DUNSTER.

62832

Above: a peaceful view of the yarn market, below: turrets and battle-ments among the trees surrounding the castle and, opposite: a view from the castle down to the yarn market, flanked by present-day parked cars.

history the castle has only ever been in the possession of two families, the De Mohuns and the Luttrells. The castle was handed over to William De Mohun by William the Conqueror after the Battle of Hastings and it remained with the De Mohun family until 1376. A small slip of parchment exists to show that in that year the right of succession to the Barony of Dunster was sold to the Lady Elizabeth Luttrell by the last surviving member of the De Mohun family, Lady Joan. The castle and estates all passed to the Luttrell family soon after Lady Joan's death in 1404. During the Civil War the castle was held first for Parliament and then for the King and by 1645 was the only place left in Somerset to fly the Royal Standard.

Coming down into the village from the castle the first thing that catches your eye is the curiously shaped building dominating the main street. This octagonal structure has a central stone pillar from which huge oak beams spread out, the roof is pyramid shaped with two gables either side of each roof section. In under the roof is evidence of its rough treatment during the Civil War – a cannonball hole can be seen in one of the beams. It is called the Yarn Market and was once the trading place for the people whose livelihood was making cloth in and around the area. It was a very busy centre for the manufacture of 'kerseymeres' which in this area were known as 'Dunsters'.

The main street of Dunster is very wide with beautiful Tudor houses displaying intricately carved oak doorways and quaint windows which in many cases are now shop fronts or tea rooms. Dunster's magnetism attracts many visitors every year but luckily the village has managed to remain unspoilt. The wide street was once the market place and the row of wooden shops or shambles which occupied the centre, until they were pulled down in 1825, would have made the street much narrower and less imposing.

The Luttrell Arms stands at the top of the street on a sharp corner, it was originally built in 1499 for the Abbot of Cleve to use as his guest house but has been an inn for at least three centuries. One of the interesting features is the way the lancet-windows are cut so an arrow could be fired at an angle as well as straight. These windows are set into a magnificent fifteenth-century porch and the whole building is swathed in Virginia Creeper which in autumn turns ruby-red and bathes the inn in colour.

Left: *The foliaged facade of the Luttrell Arms,* above: *the yarn market and,* below: *cars converge on Dunster.*

CURIOUS STONES: OLD AND NEW

E XMOOR has its share of curious stones, many date back to early Bronze Age but because of the lack of raw materials there are fewer than on some of Britain's other upland regions.

If you look at Dartmoor, with its rocky outcrops and immense tors of granite, you can understand early man making use of these readily available chunks of stone to build their circles and monuments. Exmoor, however, has no such features. The landscape is not strewn with boulders as are other moors of the South West, any stone used must first have been quarried from local sources and laboriously transported to the site.

Cairns and tumuli, ancient burial mounds, were generally constructions of haphazard piles of loose rock, and some of these can still be found on Exmoor, but early settlers would have built their dwellings mostly of perishable materials which have left little trace of their existence.

On Exmoor there remain several fine examples of ancient barrows, the prehistoric equivalent of our cemetery. Some of these are in an area known as the Chains. It is a bleak, boggy place where moisture-laden clouds from the Bristol Channel regularly deposit their rain.

The rivers Barle, Exe and West Lyn all have their source here, rising on the western edge of Exmoor and radiating outwards from this inhospitable place. The soil is very acidic, limiting the vegetation, the rainfall high and a miserable atmosphere pervades, making it a most curious part of the moor.

There is evidence of Bronze Age settlement but when you consider the damp conditions, much of the time the area being enveloped in

The Froude-Hancock Stone.

mist and cloud, you might wonder why people chose to live here. However, we know that the climate has changed, it was then much hotter and drier. Nowadays, it is unwelcoming as no other part of Exmoor is.

The Longstone, an immense monolith standing nearly nine feet high, rises from the desolate landscape like a sentinel. Its real purpose is unknown, but it could easily be an object of worship, dedicated to a pagan god and used during rituals and religious ceremonies. The mysterious round barrows of Wood Barrow, Chapman Barrows and Longstone Barrow lie dotted about. Some have been plundered by treasure hunters or archaeologists but generally they still hold their secrets locked within the mounds of earth and stone. Skeletons and artefacts buried so long ago hold a vital key to the role played by Exmoor in man's evolution.

There are some stones on Exmoor that are not so old but are still of importance. The methods by which they were erected are modern but the reasons for doing so are ancient and everlasting. They are mostly dedicated to people who have lived on Exmoor and loved the place dearly. One such is the Negus Stone near Chapman Barrows, put up in the memory of a Robin Negus who died at the age of eighteen. His father chose this particular spot because the boy loved it so much. Another, larger memorial is the Froude-Hancock Stone, an immense chunk of granite placed on West Anstey Common in 1935. It commemorates Philip Froude-Hancock, an international rugby player and renowned stag-hunter, a man of great stature who was well regarded on Exmoor.

In a mysterious corner of Exmoor stands the Sloley Stone. It is inscribed with the names of two landowners who placed it to mark the boundary of their manors at Lew Combe in 1742. Strange then that this stone should have 'wandered' to a site further south between the notoriously boggy Mole's Chamber and the ruins of the Acland Arms. This was an inn built for mine workers, now no more than a mound, its iniquitous reputation buried with it.

Outside the village of Combe Martin on the very fringe of Exmoor is a curious stone known as the Hanging Stone. The hills nearby are called Great Hangman and Little Hangman and one might suppose that this was an execution site, but this is not how this particular stone got its name. Fellow Bossiney author, Sally Jones, in her *Legends of Devon*, unravelled the mystery and discovered the tale behind the naming of the stone. Apparently a thief stole a sheep and tied it around his neck to make it easier to carry home. The animal soon became very heavy so he rested on a rock, but unfortunately for him the sheep struggled, slid over the other side of the stone and strangled the thief. You might think this extraordinary story unique but other sheep-stealers appear to have suffered this fate in other parts of the country. The legend obviously has a moral but the name is derived from the Saxon 'Stanes Hengen' meaning hanging or uplifting stones. I prefer the idea that the stone was a reminder that in those days sheep-stealing was a

The Caratacus Stone.

hanging offence!

There are many other stones in the Exmoor countryside, some with inscriptions impossible to decipher since the elements have obliterated them but in many cases the legend is just legible amidst lichen and vegetation, arousing curiosity and a longing to know what part these people played in Exmoor's history.

COW CASTLE

E XMOOR abounds with ancient barrows and earthworks, most of which have been studied by archaeologists whose explanations are, no doubt, correct but perhaps mundane. If you want to hear the more fanciful and curious answer to the question of how Cow Castle, near Simonsbath, came into being, then delving into Exmoor folklore will provide this lovely tale.

Cow Castle is situated on a low hill at the confluence of the River Barle and a little stream called White Water south east of Simonsbath. It is the site of an old hill fort or camp. But the local people see it differently. It is known to them as Ring Castle and was built by Exmoor's pixies who inhabited Exmoor. The good pixies were continuously at war with the evil mine spirits who lived beneath the forest and hills, but they were sadly no match for the devilish little goblins. So the Pixie Queen decided the time had come to free themselves from the tyranny and using all her resources commanded her subjects to build the mysterious circle. Within each stone and piece of turf they instilled the memory of some kindly deed which the Pixies had performed for the good of mankind, thus creating such forces of virtue that the demons were overwhelmed and could not penetrate the magical ring. This was not the end of the curious tale for as morning broke the mist cleared from the hilltop and ring after ring of pale yellow smoke rose out of the circle and gently floated away. These tiny rings alighted in various places all over Exmoor creating lush green circles of grass wherever they chanced to land. It is within these fairy rings that the Pixies dance in the moonlight, knowing they are safe from the evil mine spirits.

*Beneath the peaceful tapestry of fields and hedgerows in the gentle
Exmoor countryside lies a wealth of legend, mystery and folklore.*

MOLLAND CHURCH

MOLLAND Church is situated on the fringe of the southern boundary of Exmoor National Park near West Anstey Common. The interior of the church contains several unusual features. The pulpit is a complicated affair with three tiers and the pews are a motley selection of varying heights and sizes. No uniformity appears to exist in the seating arrangements here.

On the wall is a plaque, a reminder of the preparation made by the village in the event of an invasion by Napoleon in 1804 and the action to be taken depending on the 'March of the Troops'.

Molland Church – a stroll down the lane, through the iron gate and into this little house of worship is well rewarded. A singular pulpit, a delightfully eccentric collection of pews and some interesting relics await you.

To the Conductors and Overseers of the said Waggons. and Car...

Mr *John Cockram and James Withins* — Conductors

ON receiving Orders, or in case of an Enemy landing in your immediate Neighbourhood, without waiting for such Orders, you are to repair to *Molland Town* — there to take under your charge the Waggons and Carts, appointed for the Removal of the Sick and Infirm, and to conduct them by such Route, and to such Place as you shall receive Orders to do, taking care in all Cases, to avoid travelling upon the public Roads, which are to be left open for the King's Use, namely, for the Conveyance of Ammunition and Provision for the Troops, and for their March; and in order to this, if necessary, you will have proper Tools with you, for the purpose of making Breaches in Hedges, &c. You are to be very careful of all those placed under your Charge, and provide for them in the best Manner you shall be able.

N. B. The line of March (if to Somerton) is pointed out:

From Molland Town over Molland Common to Dulverton
From Dulverton cross the Roads to Wivelscombe
From Wivelscombe to Gore Inn
From Gore Inn to Langport
From Langport to Somerton

— *If the line of March is to Dartmoor:*

From Molland Town to Bishopsnympton
From Bishopsnympton to Maryansleigh
From Maryansleigh to Mashshaw
From Mashshaw to East Worlington
From East Worlington to Lapford
From Lapford to Zeal monachorum
From Zeal to Spreyton
From Spreyton to Chagford

TREWMANS, PRINTERS, EXETER.

Left: careful instructions to the 'conductors' of local waggons on their duties in the event of an invasion by Napoleon's troops. They are charged with taking the 'Sick and Infirm' to safety, while keeping off the King's Highway and breaching if necessary, any hedges with 'proper Tools'.

Above: the ornate pulpit and beautiful carving in Molland Church.

The extraordinary Pack of Cards at Combe Martin. Visitors enjoy seeing if they can spot the original 52 windows.

ON THE FRINGE OF EXMOOR

THE SCENERY at the very edge of the moor is just as spectacular as the scenery at its heart. Combe Martin is strictly speaking, outside the National Park boundary but it deserves a mention because it is so picturesque and has several curious features that capture the imagination.

The strangest house, in the shape of a house of cards, is situated in the straggling main street of the village. It was built by George Ley in the eighteenth century with his winnings from a card game. Originally it had 52 windows, though some were blocked up at a later date to avoid the dreaded window tax, each storey decreases in size as the building gets higher, chimneys sprout from every corner and there are four floors corresponding to the four suits in the pack. It was an amazing way to celebrate one's good fortune at cards, a unique monument to Lady Luck.

The village is also renowned for its silver mines and records show three tankards were fashioned from a huge cup made of Combe Martin silver, which was presented to the Lord Mayor of London in 1643. Three replicas are still used at banquets at the Mansion House today. The mines are now disused and the once-rich veins of ore which brought wealth to the village have been neglected. They have, however, left behind an unwelcome legacy. Some people fear that the shafts have badly undermined the foundations of the village.

Brooding, mysterious and, sometimes even sinister, the Valley of Rocks challenges visitors to experience its strange atmosphere and remain unmoved.

THE VALLEY OF ROCKS

T HE POET Southey summed up the splendour of this unique
corner of Exmoor when he described it as 'the very bones and
skeleton of the earth, rock reeling upon rock, stone piled upon stone, a
huge terrific mass'. R.D. Blackmore referred to the phenomenon as
the 'Devil's Cheese-ring' or the 'Devil's Cheese-knife' in his book
Lorna Doone but it was also known by a third name, the 'Devil's
Cheese-press'. But whatever it is called you cannot fail to sense the
atmosphere which surrounds the valley, especially if you visit on a day
when low cloud hangs mysteriously over the rocks.

These appear carelessly strewn, coming together in places to form
weird shapes – perhaps the distorted figure of an old crone or maybe
an animal's head. It is easy to let your imagination run riot in such a
place. You may be lucky enough to spot one of the real animals which
dwell in this barren landscape, for the valley is the haunt of wild goats.
Apparently, some years ago, they had to be removed because they but-
ted too many valuable sheep over the cliffs, but now they have been
allowed to return and can once more be seen browsing on tufts of grass
high up on craggy rocks.

What a curious yet wonderful setting this valley is for a cricket
match. The ground of the Lynton and Lynmouth Cricket Club is situated in the valley floor and the sound of leather on willow has echoed
around these rocks since 1876. It is strange indeed to see amidst such
desolate landscape a patch of verdant green – the carefully nurtured
pitch.

There is an interesting legend describing how the Valley of Rocks
was formed. In the middle of the twelfth century, so the story goes, the

Rock piled upon rock, in a barren landscape.

Lynton family lived at Lynton Castle, and this unfortunate household was under the watchful eye of the Devil himself, who at any opportunity performed malicious acts against them. Reginald Lynton, in order to break the Devil's curse, built a church at Lynmouth in honour of his chosen God. He picked the site of an old abbey, a sacred spot, which caused Satan to loosen his hold over the family. The castle collapsed, 'the cliff heaved as if in pain, and the terrible convulsions formed the Valley of Rocks, the Devil was seen scudding before the wind'.

It is an evocative tale, but unfortunately there never was a castle at Lynton nor an abbey at Lynmouth, though Lee Abbey can be seen nearby along the toll road leaving the valley towards Martinhoe. This

A towering landscape – do the rocks have their own tale to tell to those who can tune into the past?

90

'a bit of Dartmoor dropped into Exmoor by the sea.'

abbey was not built until 1850 and did not originally have religious connections. It was built on the site of an old farmhouse, the home of a Devonshire family, the Wichehalses, a name found in the pages of R.D. Blackmore's *Lorna Doone*. The Abbey has weathered well and blends comfortably with the surrounding clifftops. Ironically now, in later years, it has become a retreat, a centre for the Church of England's Christian work, but this Victorian structure could not have been the subject of the ancient legend.

Perhaps then the answer lies in another superstition, that the rocks represent people turned to stone, as if by Medusa, a punishment for dancing on the Sabbath. Looking at the valley, many ideas on how these rocks came to be in such strange formation spring to mind. It is easy to speculate endlessly as did our ancestors who told these wonderful tales.

MORE BOSSINEY BOOKS....

ABOUT EXMOOR
by Polly Lloyd
Old photographs, postcards and a tasteful blend of more modern photographs are brought to life by Polly Lloyd's imaginative writing.

UNKNOWN SOMERSET
by Rosemary Clinch and Michael Williams
A journey across Somerset, visiting off-the-beaten track places of interest. Many specially commissioned photographs by Julia Davey add to the spirit of adventure.
'*Somerset has been called the 'County of Romantic Splendour' and the two authors have explored many of the less well-known aspects of the countryside and written about them with enthusiasm.*'
Somerset and Avon Life

STRANGE SOMERSET STORIES
introduced by David Foot with chapters by Ray Waddon, Jack Hurley, Lornie Leete-Hodge, Hilary Wreford, David Foot, Rosemary Clinch and Michael Williams.
'*Publisher Michael Williams has tried to capture an essence of the West-country bizarre . . .*'
Peter John, Bath and West Evening Chronicle

LEGENDS OF SOMERSET
by Sally Jones
65 photographs and drawings
Sally Jones travels across rich legendary landscapes. Words, drawings and photographs all combine to evoke a spirit of adventure.
'*On the misty lands of the Somerset plain – as Sally Jones makes clear – history, legend and fantasy are inextricably mixed.*'
Dan Lees, The Western Daily Express

THE QUANTOCKS
by Jillian Powell with photographs by Julia Davey
'*Seen from Taunton or The Mendips, the Quantocks look timeless . . .*' Sensitive combination of words and pictures produce a delightful portrait of the area.
'*. . . a charming portrait of an area of great natural beauty and much historic interest.*'
Somerset and Avon Life

SUPERNATURAL IN SOMERSET
by Rosemary Clinch
Atmospheres, healing, dowsing, fork-bending and strange encounters are only some of the subjects featured inside these pages. A book destined to entertain and enlighten – one which will trigger discussion – certain to be applauded and attacked.

MENDIP COUNTRY
by Jillian Powell

Jillian Powell, with photographer Julia Davey, explores these famous West-country hills which stretch for some twenty miles. *'These hills are rife with history and legend . . .'*

GHOSTS OF SOMERSET
by Peter Underwood

The President of the Ghost Club completes a hat-trick of hauntings for Bossiney.

'. . . many spirits that have sent shivers down the spines over the years . . .'
Somerset County Gazette

WESTCOUNTRY MYSTERIES
introduced by Colin Wilson

A team of authors probe mysterious happenings in Somerset, Devon and Cornwall. Drawings and photographs all add to the mysterious content.

'A team of authors have joined forces to re-examine and probe various yarns from the puzzling to the tragic.'
James Belsey, Bristol Evening Post

CURIOUS BRISTOL
by Rosemary Clinch

Rosemary Clinch, who lives at Littleton-on-Severn, takes us on a fascinating tour of a city which has often led London.

E.V. THOMPSON'S WESTCOUNTRY

This is a memorable journey: combination of colour and black-and-white photography.

'Stunning photographs and fascinating facts make this an ideal book for South West tourists and residents alike – beautifully atmospheric colour shots make browsing through the pages a real delight.'
Jane Leigh, Express & Echo

We shall be pleased to send you our catalogue giving full details of our growing list of titles for Devon, Cornwall, Somerset, Dorset and Wiltshire as well as forthcoming publications. If you have difficulty in obtaining our books, write direct to Bossiney Books, Land's End, St Teath, Bodmin, Cornwall.